D1215761

PSALMS

PSALMS

Ernesto Cardenal

CROSSROAD · New York

1981
The Crossroad Publishing Company
18 East 41st Street, New York, NY 10017

Published in Spanish under the title *Salmos*
by Ediciones Carlos Lohle, Buenos Aires
Copyright © 1969 by Ernesto Cardenal

These translations copyright © 1981 by Search Press Limited

Translated by Thomas Blackburn, John Griffiths, John Heath-Stubbs,
Sylvester Houédard, Elizabeth Jennings, Peter Levi, and Tony Rudolf

Printed in the United States of America

Library of Congress Cataloging in Publication Data

Cardenal, Ernesto.
  Psalms.

   Translation of: Salmos.
   I. Blackburn, Thomas, 1916-.   II. Title.
PQ7519.C34S314   1981   861   81-1096
ISBN 0-8245-0044-X (pbk.)   AACR2

Contents

PSALMS

As on the potter's wheel

Bless the Lord, O my soul
Lord my God you are great
       You are clothed with the energy of atoms
       as with a mantle
From a cloud of whirling cosmic dust
as on the potter's wheel
you began to tease out the whorls of the galaxies
and the gas escapes from your fingers condensing and burning
and you were fashioning the stars
You made a spatterdash of planets like spores or seeds
and scattered comets like flowers
A sea of red waves was the whole planet
iron and red-hot molten rock
       rising and falling like tides
and all the water steam
its dense clouds darkening the whole earth
and it began raining and raining for centuries and centuries
     long rain for centuries on stony continents
and after aeons appeared the seas
and the mountains began to emerge
       (the earth was in labour)
growing like great beasts
and to be eroded by the water
(remaining there like the débris of these times)
       like piled-up rubble)

and the first molecule was made fecund by the power of water
    and light
and the first bacterium divided
and in the Precambrian the first tenuous transparent alga
nourished by solar energy
and the flagellates transparent as little bells of glass
or jelly-like flowers
moved and reproduced
(and from thence proceeded the creation that we know)
And thence the first sponges
and jellyfish as of plastic,
polyps — all mouth and stomach
and the first molluscs
and the first echinoderms: the starfish and sea urchin.
And at the beginning of the Cambrian, sponges
covered the whole sea-bed
making reefs from pole to pole.
And in the middle Cambrian all these died out
And the first corals flourished
filling the deep with crimson skyscrapers
In the waters of the Silurian the first pincers: sea scorpions
and at the end of the Silurian the first fish ravening
like a diminutive shark (already with jaws)
The algae have turned into trees in the Devonian
learning to breathe

casting their spores and beginning to grow in forests
and the first stems and first leaves were born.
The first lowly animals colonized the land:
scorpions and spiders fleeing the competitiveness of the sea.
Fins grow and the first amphibians appear
and fins become feet.
Soft fleshy trees grew in the Palaeozoic swamps.
There were no flowers.yet
and insects appear
dinosaurs and birds are born
and the first flowers are visited by the first bees.
In the Mesozoic the first timid mammals appear
small and warm-blooded
      They bring forth their young alive and suckle them with

                                       milk

and in the Eocene lemurs climbing on the branches
and the tarsiers with stereoscopic eyes like man's
and at the beginning of the Quaternary you created man
You give the polar bear his coat the colour of the glacier
and the Arctic fox his, the colour of snow
You make the stoat brown in summer and white in winter
and you give the praying mantis its camouflage
You camouflage the butterflies with flower-colours
You shewed the beavers how to build their dams of sticks
            and their lodges on the water

The grasshopper comes into the world knowing how to fly and
                                        sing and what its food is
and the wasp knowing how to bore into tree trunks
to lay its eggs
and the spider how to weave its web
As soon as they are hatched the storks know where north and
                                        south are
and with no-one to guide them fly in a northward direction
You gave speed to the cheetah
and suckers to the tree-frog
and a sense of smell to the moth
to find out the odour of the female in the night
                at two miles distance
and luminous organs to crustaceans
and you give telescopic eyes to the fish of the great depths
and batteries to the electric eel
You invented the mechanisms whereby flowers are fertilized
You give seeds wings to fly on the wind
membranes as if they were butterflies.
Others have down to float on the wind
or they drop like puffs
                or propellers
                or parachutes
or float on the water like ships looking for markers
and pollen always knows its precise way:

10

it does not falter on the mesh of the style
before reaching the ovule

      The eyes of all wait upon you, O Lord
        and you give to each his food in due season
You open your hand
and you fill all things living with your blessings
To the humble copepod you give its diatoms
The sea anemones (fierce and voracious flowers)
beg you for nourishment
           and you feed them
The cellophane ragworm
           begs you for food with its hungry tentacles
You give algae and crabs to the dabchick and its young
and for the dunlin you give soft molluscs.
The sparrows have no barns nor tractors
yet you give them the grains that drop from lorries
on the highroad
        on their way to the barn
And you give the nectar of flowers to the hummingbird
You give tender rice-grains to the bobolink
and fish to the kingfisher and his mate
Everyday the seagull finds his fish;
every night the owl his frogs and mice.
You prepare for the cuckoo his lunch of caterpillars
and woolly-bears

You give the crow his crickets
Insects to the cricket chirping in his burrow
You give small red berries to the barbet
and he has more berries than he can eat
The chipmunk spends the winter asleep;
when he wakes up he has his seeds handy
and you open the first flowers of spring
when the first butterflies come out of their chrysalids
You open flowers in the morning for butterflies
and you close them in the evening when they go to sleep
You open others in the night for moths
that spend the whole day asleep in dark crannies
and begin to fly at nightfall
You wake the bumblebees from their winter sleep
the same day that you open the catkins of the willow

I will sing to the Lord as long as I live
I will write him psalms
        May my song please him
Bless the Lord O my soul
        Alleluia

Translated by John Heath-Stubbs

Blessed the man

Blessed the man who says no to the party
who will not join committees
and follow the line
who will not sit down with gangsters
or generals in council
plotting war to surpass all war
Blessed the man who will not report
brother or sister
neighbour or friend
Blessed the man who coughs at commercials
defies their radio
and knows their slogans for lies
      He grows by the river of life

Translated by John Griffiths

Do you think I'm ambitious?

Lord
do you think
I'm ambitious?
that I'd like to be a millionaire
dream
of becoming a member of the cabinet
and maybe prime minister?
Lord
I'm not even interested in politics
I'd never accept a peerage
Not
that they're likely to offer me one
I don't own this house
I don't have a bank account
I haven't even got
an insurance policy
The only thing I have got
is you

If they were all like me
instead of leaving things to the government
would this
be a more interesting country?

Translated by Sylvester Houédard

O God of vengeance

When O
God
are you going to let
your divine vengeance
be seen?
How long
are you going to let
the party stay in power?
How much longer do we have to
go on listening
to their clichés?

Or maybe you've changed?
Don't you care now
about victims of exploitation?
are you happy
seeing the masses oppressed?
Do you actually want people to think
you are
a blind force of nature?

something atavistic
left over in the subconscious?

You
the famous inventor of the brain

You think up this elegant system
with auditory nerve endings
and you can't even hear?

You work out
the neurophysics of sight
and you can't see?

Has your databank
been stopping print-outs
of our thoughts?

   Haven't you even taped
   what we've been saying?

and you're the guru
that brought us wisdom
the zen master
of bliss without tranquillizers

Lord

you can't abandon people
not
when you see them like this

18

there just has to be a day
when law-courts stop being
the last place we'd look
for justice

or

you wouldn't have done all that
to protect the partisans
we'd
all have been liquidated
you
wouldn't have bothered
when they were hunting us down
and
the only thing that kept us
on the run
was you

no

you can't have switched sides
you're
the one defence there is
against the system

it's only you
could turn their own guns
against them
trap them
in their own
political blunders
and
wipe them
out

Translated by Sylvester Houédard

The wretched of the earth

With our own ears we have heard
the story from our fathers' lips:
the victories
                in ancient days
            because we did not put our faith in weapons,
            did not depend on tanks for victory

But now you have forsaken us,
given aid and comfort to
their governing bureaucracies,
subsidized their party leaders,
propped up corrupt régimes

We are the displaced persons
            the refugees
            the stateless ones
We are the ka-tsetniks
            condemned to forced labour
            condemned to gas chambers

burned in the crematoria
we are anonymous ashes

                We are the children of Auschwitz
                    the children of Buchenwald
                        of Belsen
                        Dachau

They used our skin for lampshades
our fat for bars of soap

They dragged us off
(and you let them),
sheep to the slaughter,
to the gas-chambers

They deported us
and you looked on

They put us up for sale:
there was no buyer

Piled into railway cars
we travelled like cattle
to fields lit up
and ringed with barbed wire

packed in lorries
for the gas-chambers

naked we went
into gas-chambers
upstairs and downstairs
in the gas-chambers

and they locked the doors
and put out the lights

and you veiled us with the shadow of death

and nothing survived
but mountains
of clothes
toys
shoes

And if we had forgotten
the name of our God in heaven
and turned to new leaders
would you not have known?

You who know the secrets of
the heart
have no need
for Secret Services

Every day they called the roll
so we might hear the names
of those marked down for gas-ovens that day

all day we're made
ready for death
sheep for the slaughter

you dumped us naked in the range
of the flame-throwers

They have wiped your people off the earth's face
your people exist no longer in geography
We wander from country to country without passports
with no means to identify ourselves

And now you are hidden, God

Why do you hide your face?

God, our God, why have you forgotten
the wretched of the earth?

rise, God,
rise, come
            help us,
        for God's
        sake,
        yours

Translated by Tony Rudolf

Why have you left me?

Lord O Lord my God
why have you left me?
I am a caricature of a man
People think I am dirt
       they mock me in all the papers

I am encircled
       there are tanks all round me
Machine-gunners have me in their sights
       there is barbed wire about me
       electrified wire
I am on a list
I am called all day
They have tattooed me
       and marked me with a number
They have photographed me behind the barbed wire
All my bones can be counted
       as on an X-ray film
They have stripped me of my identity
They have led me naked to the gas-chamber
They have shared out my clothes and my shoes
I call for morphine
       and no one hears me
In my straitjacket I cry out
I scream all night in the mental home

in the terminal ward
in the fever hospital
in the geriatric ward
in an agony of sweat in the psychiatric clinic
In the oxygen tent I suffocate
I weep in the police cell
in the torture chamber
in the orphanage

I am contaminated with radioactivity
no one comes near me
for I am contagious

Yet
I shall tell my brothers and sisters
about you
I shall praise you in our nation
and my hymns will be heard
in a great generation
The poor will go to a banquet
and our people will give a great feast
the new people
yet to be born

Translated by John Griffiths

Answer me when I call

Answer me when I call
God of my innocence
You will free me from the torture chamber
the concentration camp
the dark cell of my agony

How long must we suffer them
bullies and leaders
in all their stupidity?
How long must we suffer their empty talk
propaganda
all propaganda?

Many ask
who will free us from their bombs
their nuclear submarines, their rocket launchers?
Lord brighter than a thousand bombs
look at us
and shine on us

Our hearts sing when you stir them
your joy is greater than their wine
all the wine at their banquets

I shall sleep when my head touches the pillow
nightmares will not trouble me
I shall not see as they do their victims accusing them
I need no tranquillizers, no sleeping pills
You Lord are my comforter
you are my strength

Translated by John Griffiths

Do me justice Lord

Do me justice my Lord God
because I am innocent
Trusted you not leaders indecent
And perjured, perverted and mad

Defend me from false evidence
because I have never been
at their banquets, collusive, obscene
party to organized no sense
I do not keep their company
Nor are they familiar with me

Innocent I think that I am
Let me be close to your altar Lord
Not to blasphemers of the word
the attaché cases of crime
the attritions not found but lost
in a circumstanced blessed ghost
No wonder I praise your name

Translated by Thomas Blackburn

They freed me from the mafia

Lord it is in you I trust
that never ever shall I be lost but inherit
the earth for your hands freed me from the mafia
Into your hands I commend my spirit

You have freed me O Lord God
who celebrate not lies but things as they are
and hate worshippers of empty images
party lines written on neat pages
You are the one my hope rests upon

And did not hand me over to the secret police
but delivered me from the camp of concentration

Pity me God for I am in trouble,
While they are at their riotous celebration
Dissolving the ego in alcohol
we weep in the night in a species of hell
In a ransacked house there is an empty place
at the dining room table; my cup is bitter and full
as I await their knock at the door
and am rejected by other people
as if I was a ghost and did not exist
All night they blaspheme us on the radio
and the technocrats hatch their plots also

I would not be Lord among the lost
but in silence among the just celebrate the just
You God are my hope and my shelter
And among the mutables do not falter or alter

Translated by Thomas Blackburn

You made it public Lord

You made it public
Lord
You announced
you were on our side
Now
you're the only ally
we have left

You heard the announcement
The authorities
have fulfilled their threat
They've assumed full
and unlimited powers
so
we'll be expecting you
to open hostilities
any time from now

If what you claim is true
and your military capability
really is greater than theirs
the time
has come to use it

Lord
this
is where you come in

There's no question we attacked them
before they started this witch-hunt
We hadn't even been plotting to
before they sent us to prison

The truth is
these thugs set a trap
and we just fell in

The situation is
there's only you
left to get rid of the dictator
now they've put into operation
his scheme
for exploiting
the lowest paid workers

What could I do?
Those were highly paid witnesses
committing perjury
When they've finished typing the final draft of my confession

34

all the interrogators need
is for me to sign and I'll be admitting
conspiracy espionage sabotage and

Lord
what's the longest
a system can last
when it's rotten as this with corruption?
When's the soonest
something can
step in
take over
and
fix these fixers?

How long
can you pretend to be neutral
standing there
watching it happen
listening to them laughing at us
joking about you
and preparing for war
pretending
it's the safest way to guarantee peace?

Lord
how can you sit there
silent
tuning in to radio propaganda
and chasing their one-party channels?
Listen
I tell you they're preparing for war
and it's time
you got moving

If
that is
you're going to bother
at all

It couldn't be you're getting a taste
for stories about prison-camps tortures and sadists?
that you found it amusing
they called a press conference
to announce the bank holiday
in honour of our destruction?
Because it was us you know that they meant when they said:
all opposition to the party's political aims
has finally
been eliminated

36

Lord
have you even got a plan
to put into operation
or
are you planning
to celebrate too?

>And
>it would have been
>so easy
>for you to eliminate them
>and give us
>a bit of a holiday
>O
>God
>why

do I spend my life
writing
poems
to
you?

Translated by Sylvester Houédard

Hear my cries

Lord listen to what I'm saying
hear my cries
and my I-can't-stand-it
You never plot with dictators
your politics are straight
They don't fool you with slick campaigns
you're not behind them
the con-men
the party bosses

Their words are dead
you know there's nothing in them
their press-releases and statements

Their speeches are honeyed with peace
they drip love and kindness
and their stock-piles grow the faster

They hold peace conferences
more they could not
They talk of friendship among nations
In secret they prepare weapons of war
of utter destruction

Their wavelengths dance with lies
evil songs in the darkness
Their desks are heavy with plots
Lord preserve me from their scheming

Their mouths are machine-guns
and their tongues deal death
Punish them Lord
Make dust of their projects
and cheap ideas
of all their memoranda

When the siren wails the last warning
you will be with me
You will be my refuge
my strength and deep shelter

You will bless the man
who shuns their slogans and campaigns
their hand-outs and all they say
You will circle him with armour
and shield him with all your love

Translated by John Griffiths

Listen everybody

Listen everybody, listen to me
There is no cause for trust in any bank
nor security in an insurance policy
They are the extremity of nonentity
However much you may deny the grave
despite all cheques it's what you must have
They claimed power, they named a city
after their name, property they had stolen
Bloat-eyed, statued, bronzed and swollen
and now no more than faint nonentity
So do not for the mighty care a straw
they teeter on the edge of nothingness
and are life's posturing antithesis
their medals but bits of metal, nothing more

But the man of great honour does not understand
the fat and heavy-chested dictator,
that he is fattened like a sacrifice for
his journey to the mysterium of world's end

Translated by Thomas Blackburn

Jerusalem is a heap of rubble

O God so far
the blood of your people flowed from street to street
Jerusalem is a heap of rubble under our feet
It poured into the sewers where the rats are

Propaganda makes us into a joke
all the slogans of hatred keep wide awake

How long will you hate us Lord?
Burn us by your anger abhorred
like a nuclear storm never tired
Must unbelievers ever say
Where is now their God, has he gone away?

Hear the groans of the prisoners
and the sigh of those condemned to forced labours
and those to death sentenced
the prayer of those in camps who are not mentioned

And we your people will praise you without end
and the generations hear you and understand

Translated by Thomas Blackburn

Free me Lord

Free me Lord
from the S.S. and the N.K.V.D. from the F.B.I. and the G.N.
Free me from war councils and their vicious regimen

You are the judge of all judges
You judge the ministers of justice
You are the energy from which all justice is

Defend me then from falsity
the exiled, the lonely, the deported
the accused of espionage and found guilty
and to forced labour transported

But the weapons of God more terrible are
and 'sub specie aeternitas' accurate
than the judgment of those judges whose judgment will occur

I will celebrate you in my singing
where you sit on your seat in the high court of no thing

Translated by Thomas Blackburn

Lord I'm appealing to you

Lord
I'm appealing to you
because you claim
to be the God of justice
and these aren't law-courts
These political tribunals
aren't concerned about truth
all they do
is check how far
we know the myths
of party dogma

Do you think
I'd object to night-time interrogations
if the floodlights
and lie-detectors
were yours?
I'd plead guilty then
to the crime of not listening
to commercials and
radio propaganda

The only thing
I tune into
is your word

I'm seeing things
through your eyes
and counting on you for protection
Your political wing
is the only shelter left now
for opponents
of the dictator

With his mafiosi
getting us both
in their machine-gun sights
he can have spies all round me
secret police
watching round the clock
and I'll sleep easy
you're the one
they'll be confronting

and they won't win
not

with you to liberate us
from these bankers
these businessmen who've lived
a bit too long in exclusive clubs

48

where the deep-freeze
is crammed
and the dog gets fed
on left-overs of caviare
Not
that I was a member
remember
          -ing
what you're to provide
after this
long night's
over

Translated by Sylvester Houédard

Help, Lord

Lord who do you think is going to
liberate us
if you don't?

Certainly not these politicians
They spent the election exploiting each other's mistakes
and since then they've spent it
thinking up lies on the radio
they're not interested in anything
outside party conflict
it's either one-up to them
or the others get smeared in the media

Mind you
the lies are clever
they pay experts to think them up
and there's one truth sacred at party HQs:
power depends on
propaganda

> But now
>   says the Lord
> it's my turn
> I've been watching the poor
>   and their oppression

I've listened to them groaning
     as each party in power
     continues to exploit them
and now I'm going to give them
the freedom they long for

Well
that's God's propaganda

The riot squads are armed
and no sign of them being laid off
The tanks are still there
so are the machine guns
that's no sign of them ending
insults and provocations

After each incident
it still amuses our leaders
to pin up the new medals
Tonight in the Club
there'll be the usual toasts
to another success
while
you can still hear the tears in the slums

Not
of course
if you spend your life
at cocktail parties

Translated by Sylvester Houédard

Lord it's incredible

Lord
it's incredible
you've done it
you've actually done it
it's on the news
      'The military have
      finally accepted defeat
      and the dictator has stepped down from power
      the well-known portrait
      so much in evidence all over the country
      no longer looks down from every wall
      Many of the commemorative plaques put up by the party
      have begun to disappear
      and the squares in all the main cities
      are reported to be littered
      with fragments of statues toppled overnight
      by the people
      Old street names are being put back
      and newspapers on sale this morning
      have uniformly managed
      to avoid printing his name'

Lord
can a régime be wiped out
just like that?
their names obliterated

their memory
relegated to history books?
could the time ever come
when we had governments like yours
all over the world
real justice
for people everywhere
parliaments
that took the poor into consideration
courts
that actually listened to their complaints
police
who didn't just shrug
when their corpses
are found murdered?
        It's only that sort of hope
        keeps me going
        in this place

Lord
you used to be the great liberator
there was a time
you'd have had this barbed wire
all cut away by now
Just how much longer do you intend
leaving us in this concentration camp?

If you got us out
do you think we'd forget you
during the V-day celebrations?
Well — a bit maybe
after peace came
and we could sing in freedom

Lord
what about getting workers
in armament factories
to take over the works
turn the guns against the employers
get the police
to change sides
and make the leaders
face their own firing squads?

Nowadays
if you want to be famous and get a medal
all you do is think up
a new way of exploiting people
with luck you even end up
embalmed in the party mausoleum

God
if there were only a way

that would shift them off their pedestals
we could some way show them up for what they **are**
make the people
see
they're only tin gods

Now
that really would be
a taste of their own dirty tactics
if you did it

You might even
find it worth while
Your own credibility
is wearing pretty thin
with dictators taking over everywhere
Do you know
on this transistor
there isn't a station left
where you can escape party broadcasts?

Did you hear them again
last night
having another party
at the headquarters
The windows

look over the camp
we always see when they're lit up

You know to them
your name is just an abstract concept
and
this word 'justice'
they can't stop using it
they print it in capital letters
on every manifesto
and yet
they can't issue a statement to the press
that isn't designed to deceive us

Well
people know it's all propaganda and lies
but it's a more effective
instrument of oppression
than spies and machineguns everywhere
they really think now
they'll get away with it
Lord
isn't that all the more reason
for you not letting them

      Look at this prison
      at the whole system

you can see at a glance who's innocent
and who needs your protection
You can see
it's like orphans
once their parents are shot
there's only you to depend on
there's only you can
break up their net-work
dismantle the military machine
You're the only option we've got
in this political nightmare

Eternity is a long time to be in power Lord
listening
to the downtrodden and destitute
I suppose you've found out
that when you keep them waiting long enough
they don't only treat people like tools
they get to thinking they've taken your place

And that's the moment to choose
to show them
that you
are
you

Translated by Sylvester Houédard

When Israel left the ghettos

When Israel came at last
out of Egypt's concentration camps and when
the ghettos which had imprisoned us closed in
the mountains skipped like lambs
                    and hills were like kids
                                        then
        and every terror seemed past

        Lord, we beg you to
do this but not for us, for your glorious name
'Where is their God?' the unbelievers exclaim
Their own are politicians, film stars who scream
        from all advertising can do

        They have mouths which will not speak,
ears which won't hear, eyes which refuse to see
and noses not used for smelling. Pure fantasy
are these. Men who create gods in this way
        fool those who likewise seek

Translated by Elizabeth Jennings

Their shares are grass

Well
it is great
to make a million
on the stock exchange
but
what do you get
for your shares?
They've only lasted
in the end
like grass
in a summer drought

Of course
it's fun
to be rich
to be
a movie star
to get
top ratings on TV
and seeing people read the papers
when it's your name
splashed on page one
and eating at places
recommended
in the good food guide

but
the media won't run you that long
Make it with the smart set
and you're lucky
if some graduate
mentions you tomorrow in his thesis
      they'll all toss you
      when summer's over
      on the bonfire

You think it's different
being a famous scientist?
you wait and see
where technical progress
is leading us

Politics?
take this party leader
will he be in long?
You'll go looking one day for him
in the palace
and you'll find the place
taken over by pacifists

Join them?
Before long.
they'll have the number of concentration camps
doubled
not with these tortures
something more refined
the New Method
of investigation

Give them power
and they'll stay up half the night
refining
old methods of control
That gives them the other half
for improving
the efficiency of
exploitation

They'll all be left looking idiots
when the Lord cuts off the power

Stepping up production in
armaments

only means more weapons
to use against them
One day
political system
are going to be something
that happened in the past
the things they budget for
won't help then

It's the same on a world scale
Chair the summit conference today
and tomorrow
it's like being last year's daisies

     You ever watch
     the way
     smoke dissipates?
     Well
     that's imperialist expansionism

a bit ahead
of our time

Today for instance
they've bugged your house

tapped the phone
and put you in the hourly checks to central
They'll start rigging the trial any day
now agreement's reached
on each
of our sentences

       There could still just be time though
       Lord
       to see we didn't reach the dock
       to get us
       through this police net

       like

you walk down town
the main square
is one big Christmas tree
only it's his face
decorates it
pictures
plastered everywhere
branching off
down every side street
you walk back

they've gone
you look for his name
it isn't there
you go up to people
you ask them
and
no one
is even
allowed
to mention him

Translated by Sylvester Houédard

You will find no joy unless you stay with me

These words were said to me and you:
'You will find no joy unless you stay with me'
Film stars, politicians, dictators too
mean nothing to us. We don't want to read or see
their newspapers. In short, we'll have nothing to do
       with what their parties tell us is true.

    Nor will we listen ever
to slogans or jargon, to pompous broadcasts or
TV commercials. We will dress in our own way
We won't eat in their restaurants or buy in a store
which belongs to them. We won't listen to what they say
       at their banquets and feasts. We will never

    play even the smallest part
in their bloodthirsty toasts. Only one leader is ours
In our Lord's Promised Land we have already been given
a beautiful plot to tend. Farm laws, of course,
have been changed in what to us is an earthly Heaven
       Lord, you beat in our heart,

    are present in every cell
of our bodies. All that we are leaps for delight
Wherever we go, we know we shall find you there

You surround us with love when we fall asleep at night
and in every dream we have you also share
    O we bless you and wish you well

Translated by Elizabeth Jennings

I call out in the night

De profundis clamo ad te domine
Out of the dark night of concentration
In the voice of extreme darkness and of desolation
I question you as to my destiny

My sins are many but you pardon sins
You are not implacable like them in their investigations
But pardon those who admit abominations
I trust in the Lord and not in slogans
nor in the keening of the radio
that is with a party line synonymous
God in your dwelling place look down on us
You freedom are from attritions, from ego

Translated by Thomas Blackburn

By the waters of Babylon

By the waters of Babylon
we sit and we weep
remembering thee O Sion
in a Babylonian landscape
the lights shining in the river
the glare of night-clubs and bars
hearing Babylonian music
under Sion's quiet stars

On the willows of the river
we hang up our guitars
and weep by the willow, the willow
as Babylon's prisoners
They ask us to sing in our language
'Something native' from Sion
But away from our own country
how could we ever begin

Let my tongue shrivel up
and my lungs, cancer infect them
if I do not remember you
O my Jerusalem
Night there, a crust and water
is far far preferable
to this armed Babel, its slaughter

May your children unserviceable
spawn of laboratories
be dashed both son and daughter
on mineral verities

Translated by Thomas Blackburn

Praise the Lord

Praise the Lord in your infinite variety all creatures,
minute and enormous in your verity
whose particular and unique features
are the context of his glory and his fecundity
Praise the Lord nebulae like grains of dust
silhouetted and fixed on photographic plates
Sirius, that dog star and his confederates
Arcturus, Antares, Aldebaran, the red bull
God's cup brimming over and ever full
Praise the Lord you his meteorites and comets
In your elliptical orbits and made planets
Praise the Lord atoms and molecules
Protons and electrons and all the stars
the minute protozoa, in their liquid, the radiolaria
Praise the Lord cetaceans and atomic submarines
for you are of God's mind in your particulars
Birds, the eagle and wren, the aeroplanes
and prisms in emerald copper sulphate
in the electronic microscope infinite
Coloured flowers blooming at the bottom of the sea,
diatoms and the diadems of the Antilles
Like a rose of diamonds, let all these
and the unended maritime fauna
praise the Lord, and the Tropic of Cancer
storms of the North Atlantic and the Humboldt current,

the dark, sweating forests of the Amazon
the shining island jewels of the South Ocean
volcanoes and lagoons and the Caribbean
behind the silhouettes of the infinite palm
democratic republics, the United Nations
praise the Lord as even for police is appropriate
the students, the young, the beautiful,
His glory surpasses the heavens, it is bountiful
telescope and microscope seeing near and far
It is he who has made the people plentiful
Who would not yield to the Lord the word hosanna?

Translated by Thomas Blackburn

Galaxies chant the glory of God

Galaxies chant the glory of God
      Arcturus twenty times the sun's magnitude
Antares four hundred and eighty-seven times the sun's brilliance
and Sigma in Dorado brilliant as three hundred thousand suns
and Alpha in Orion who is equal   to twenty-seven million suns
Aldebaran who is fifty million miles across
      Alpha in the Lyre three hundred thousand light-years distant
the Nebula in the Ox-herd two hundred million light-years distant
proclaim the works of his hands.

Their language is without words
(it is not like political slogans)
      but it is not UNHEARD
The galaxies are sending mystery waves of radio
and the cold hydrogen of interstellar space
is full of waves of vision and of waves of music
From intergalactic emptiness the fields of magnetism
chant into our radio-telescopes
(and it may be there are civilizations
           transmitting messages
to the antennae of our radios)
There exist a billion galaxies in the knowable universe
turning like roundabouts
      and like musical tops.
The sun goes about his gigantic orbit
around the constellation of the Archer
      — he is like a bridegroom leaping forth from his chamber

moving surrounded by his planets at seventy-two thousand miles

                                           an hour

towards the constellations Hercules and the Lyre
(in a hundred and fifty million years he completes his circle)
and he does not depart by one inch from his orbit.

The Laws of God quiet the subconscious
        they are as perfect as the law of gravity
his words are like the parabolas of comets
his decrees are like the centrifugal whirling of the galaxies
his statutes are the statutes of the stars
        which keep their positions for ever
                           and their velocities
                           and their respective distances
and cross one another in their courses a thousand thousand times
                           without collision
The judgments of God are just
                 they are not like propaganda
They are more valuable than dollars
                 and affairs of commerce
Save me from the pride of money
                 and of political power
and I shall be free of crimes
        and of the great sin
and be pleased with the words of my poems
        O God of my freedom.

Translated by Peter Levi

Praise the Lord

Praise the Lord in his cosmos
Praise him in his sanctuary
Praise him with a radio-signal
    100,000 million light-years away
Praise him in the stars
                in inter-stellar space
Praise him in the galaxies
                 in inter-galactic space
Praise him in atoms
             in inter-atomic space
Praise him on violin and flute
                  on the saxophone
Praise him with clarinet and horn
    with cornet and trombone
        on alto-sax and trumpet
Praise him with viola and cello
        on piano and harpsichord
Praise him with blues and jazz
                with an orchestra
Praise him with spirituals
        with soul-music and Beethoven's fifth
        with marimbas and guitars
Praise him with discs and cassettes
        with high-fi systems
        and quadraphonic sound

Let everything that draws breath praise him
                    Alleluia!
Let all living cells praise the Lord
                    Alleluia!
                              Praise the Lord!

Translated by John Griffiths